Talking Hands

TALKING HANDS

*An Introduction to Communicating
with People who are Deaf*

Devised and written by **Harry Jones**
and **Lisle Willis**

Foreword by **Polly Elwes**

Drawings by Alan Davidson

Based on the Tyne Tees Television Series

STANLEY PAUL/LONDON

STANLEY PAUL & CO LTD

3 Fitzroy Square, London W1

AN IMPRINT OF THE  HUTCHINSON GROUP

London Melbourne Sydney Auckland
Wellington Johannesburg Cape Town
and agencies throughout the world

First published 1972

*This book has been set in Linotron Imprint type and
printed in Great Britain by Flarepath Printers Ltd., St. Albans,
Herts., and bound by William Brendon, Tiptree, Essex*

ISBN 0 09 113620 2 (cased)
ISBN 0 09 113621 0 (paperback)

Contents

To Arthur E. Clifford,
the Director of Programmes,
who saw the possibilities of the series,
and gave us the go-ahead

Foreword

In the past, whenever I had seen deaf people talking to each other, I'd always thought to myself how clever they must be to talk in what appeared to be such a terribly complicated way. Of course, like many of us, I'd learnt the alphabet for finger-spelling at school, not from any pure motive, I'm afraid, but solely to send messages to my classmates when the teacher's back was turned! But, when it came to the rest of the hand movements that deaf people used when they 'talked', they all seemed far, far too difficult for me!

I suppose all of us feel sorry for people who are disabled in some way, and each of us, for personal reasons, has sympathy in one particular direction or other. But, of all human handicaps, I do think that deafness is the one that gets the least understanding and sympathy. We all know how irritating and exhausting it can be, bellowing at someone who is hard of hearing. After a while, we even give up trying! And, as for those who are born deaf, we look upon them as people apart. They are different from us, so we feel shy and inhibited, and they embarrass us. I know this is how I felt myself, until a girl friend of mine had a deaf baby, and then I began to become interested in the care and teaching of the deaf.

This is one of the reasons why I was so pleased when Tyne Tees Television invited me to take part in TALKING HANDS, and, to my surprise, I found that learning the sign language wasn't anything like as difficult and complicated as I had previously thought. In fact, while we were making the programmes, the crew in the television studio were all signing away and finger-spelling like mad!

They found it easy and interesting to learn, as I'm sure you will, too. Only a little effort on your part is needed, and the rewards for making that effort are well worth while, as I know you will quickly discover.

Deafness is a terrible social handicap, and this is your opportunity to do something positive about it.

POLLY ELWES

Introduction

From the very earliest days, when man first started to communicate with his fellows through the medium of speech, those whose hearing was impaired, either from birth or through some later accident, had to devise and improvise an alternative method of communication. This had to be visual, with the hands playing such an important part that they virtually became Talking Hands, and, today, nearly 20,000 deaf people in this country use their hands in this manner to communicate with each other.

Some people whose hearing is normal have learned to 'talk' in the same way, so that they, too, can communicate with deaf people. But, to most of us, this TALKING HANDS language can seem alien and remote, not only a foreign language but almost as mysterious as a language from the far away planets.

Deaf people, once they are outside the circle of others who communicate in the same way as they do, can feel very isolated, cut off, and often lonely. Because their disability doesn't show outwardly, they look like other people, and so, when they are not ignored, they can often be misunderstood, or even ridiculed for their lack of hearing. What a wonderful thing it would be, therefore, if more of 'us' – the people who can hear – took the trouble to learn to communicate with them on their own terms, and on their own level. It may be a little chat with the old lady down the street, the workmate on the next bench, the young mother busily shopping in the supermarket, or possibly the regular in the local on the corner. We would, indeed, be opening up a whole new world, not only for them, but also for ourselves!

That is what this book sets out to do in as simple and practical a way as possible, to teach us how to turn our hands into talking hands. The deaf will be able to understand what we are saying to them by a combination of three methods:

a) by watching our mouth as we talk to them, and lip-reading;

b) by watching our hands and body as we sign to them; and, lastly,

c) when no sign exists for what we want to say, by watching our hands as we finger-spell words.

Earlier, all this was likened to a foreign language, but it is not as intimidating as it might appear at first. Because it is a visual language, there are no complicated grammatical rules to learn, no awkward tenses and no difficult declensions. All you have to remember are the twenty-six letters of the manual alphabet, and then the signs themselves, and how to fit one to the other, to convey the sense you intend.

Because the accent is on the practical, all the signs are given, not in isolation, but within the context of an actual coversation. The only exception to this rule is when one sign is complementary to another – for example, 'good' and 'bad' are linked, both in sense and signing – and, even though only one of them is used in the conversation itself, it is convenient to learn both of them together.

There are also numerous revision sections, which we've called Hand Talk, so that you can gain experience of ringing the changes upon the signs you've already learned, putting them together to convey different meanings. And, as a further aid to this, the signs are arranged in alphabetical order at the back of the book.

Conversation 1

EVA, *who is deaf, works as an alteration hand in a small tailoring factory.* DAVID GRAY, *the Social Worker with the Deaf for the Local Authority in whose area* EVA *lives, has asked her to alter a jacket for him. Today he is calling at her place of work to see if the jacket is ready. When he talks to* EVA, *he both speaks aloud and signs.*

DAVID: **How are you?**
EVA: Very well, Mr. Gray.
　　[*She finger-spells his name.*]
DAVID: Please, **Where** is **my** jacket?
　　[*He both mimes putting on jacket and finger-spells the word.*]
EVA: **I know.**
　　[*She takes his jacket from a garment rail and passes it to him.*]
DAVID: Yes, **you** know.
　　[*He tries on the jacket and is very pleased with it.*]
　　I **like** it. **How much** is it?
EVA: **£1.10 new pence.**
　　[DAVID *nods his agreement, takes out his wallet and pays for the alteration.*]
DAVID: **Thank you.** You **finger-spell** good.
EVA: You **sign** good.

In the above dialogue, the words or groups of words for which there are signs are those which are printed in **bold type**. The remaining words in this conversation, and in any of the subsequent ones – apart from those for which finger-spelling is indicated, or for signs which have already been used – are unimportant, and are added mainly to make the sense of the conversation clearer.

Indeed, when you are learning to talk to the deaf, you must always think in short, simple sentences, leaving out the inessentials. The words you use should be incapable of having more than one meaning, and put together in the simplest form, almost as if you were writing a telegram.

Something else to remember is that this is a living

language, and so cannot remain static. Not only are new signs being added all the time, but old ones are changing their meaning. Again, there are certain local variations, all of which means it is difficult to be dogmatic about signing. What we have done in this book is to choose those signs which can be most easily understood nationally, and, if there has been a choice as to which one to include, we have chosen that one which we think is most graphic and most easily understood.

Before starting to learn any of these signs, however, let's first look at the alphabet needed for finger-spelling. Many people already know this, having learned it when they were Boy Scouts or Girl Guides, and so they will only need to revise it. For those of you to whom it's new, it won't prove a mammoth task. In less than half an hour, you'll have mastered the essentials, and, from then on, all you'll need is practice to build up confidence.

A friend learning with you, so you can take turns in both sending and receiving, will be a tremendous help, both in accustoming the mind to watching the fingers, and in helping each of you to read the words more easily.

Finger-spelling

Left hand
This should be held with the fingers slightly apart, so that the hand is relaxed, and in such a position that the person to whom you are sending can see it easily.

Right hand
This, which does most of the work, moves towards the left hand, making the letters smoothly and clearly.

The Alphabet

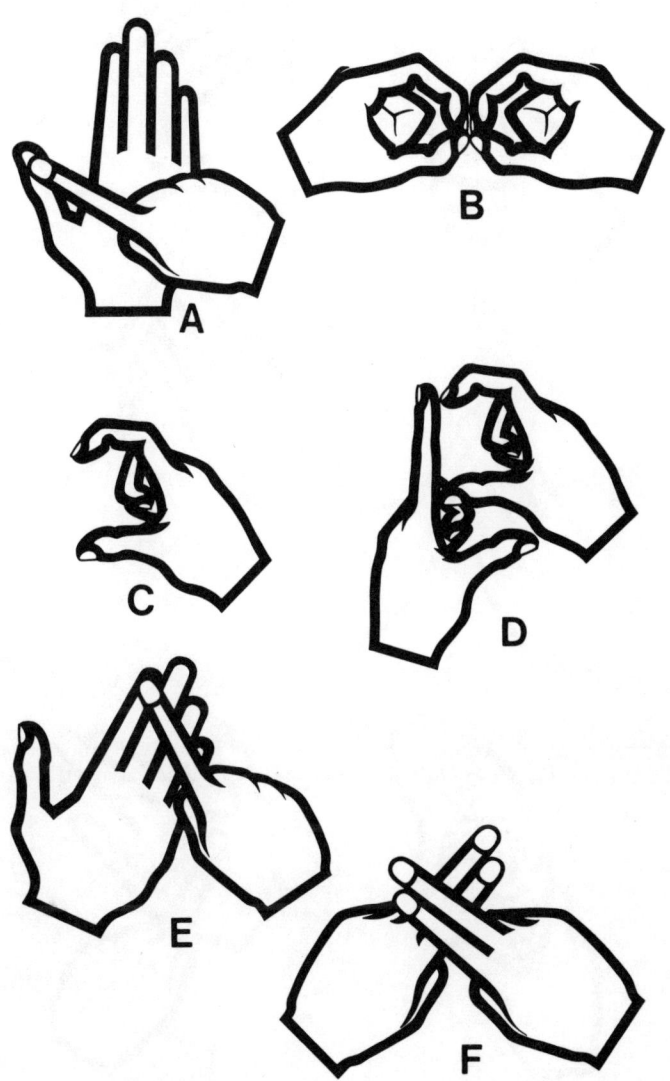

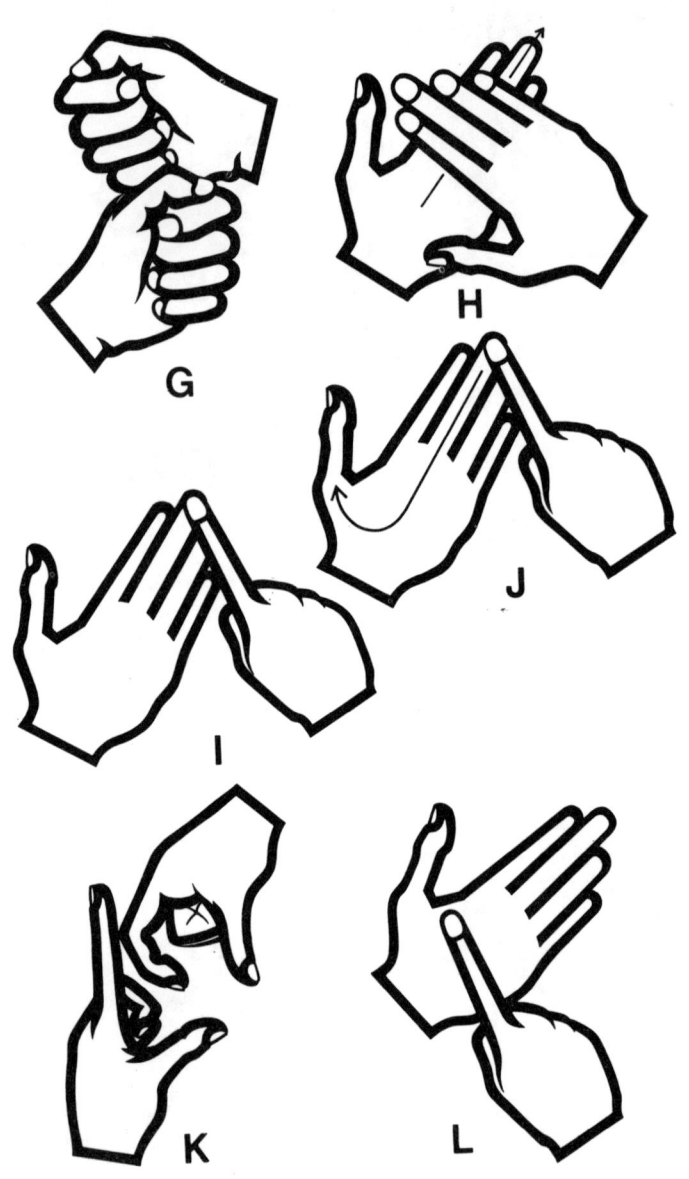

G

H

I

J

K

L

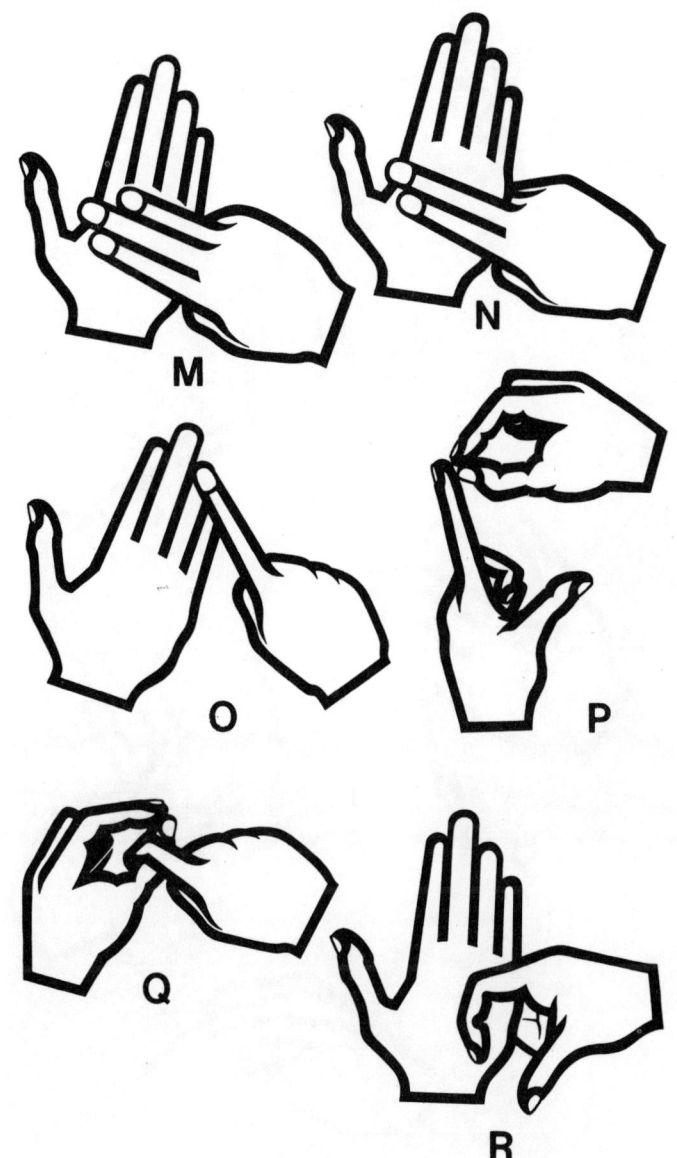

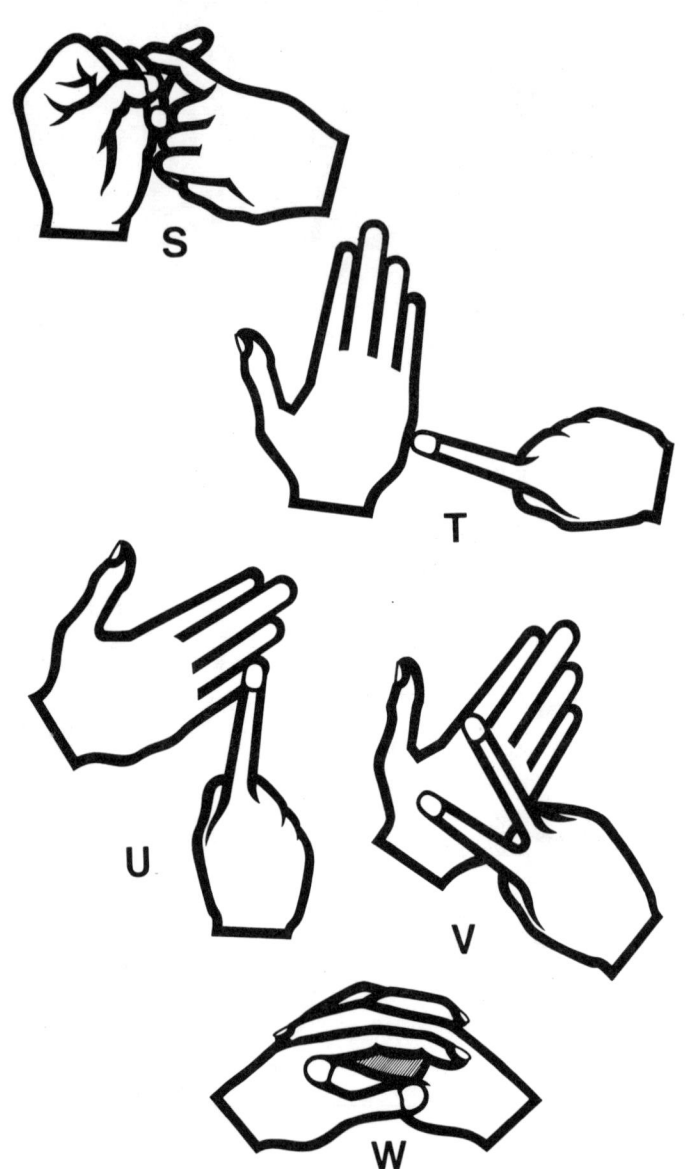

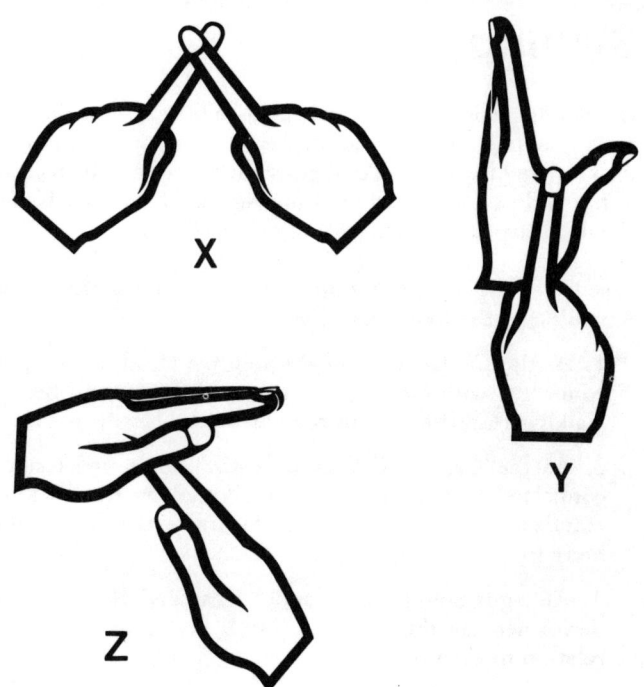

X

Y

Z

Signing

In signing, it is the arms and hands which do most of the work, moving either in relation to each other, or in relation to the head and the torso. To help you to memorise which parts of the body are involved in which signs, we have devised a Head, Heart and Hands system of classification.

Based on the drawing opposite, we can classify signs according to the following rules:

1. As the Centre of Thought is in the Head, most signs connected with *thinking* processes will be formed by the Talking Hands acting in relation to the Head.

2. As the Centre of Feeling is the Heart, most signs connected with *feelings* will be formed by the Talking Hands acting in relation to the Heart, or that part of the body in which it is located.

3. All signs not classified under Head and Heart will be performed by the Talking Hands and arms acting in relation to each other.

It must be stressed, however, that these three 'rules' are not always true. They are stated merely as a guide to memorising the signs, and as this book progresses, the signs which do conform to the rules will be classified under Head, Heart and Hands.

Head, Heart and Hands

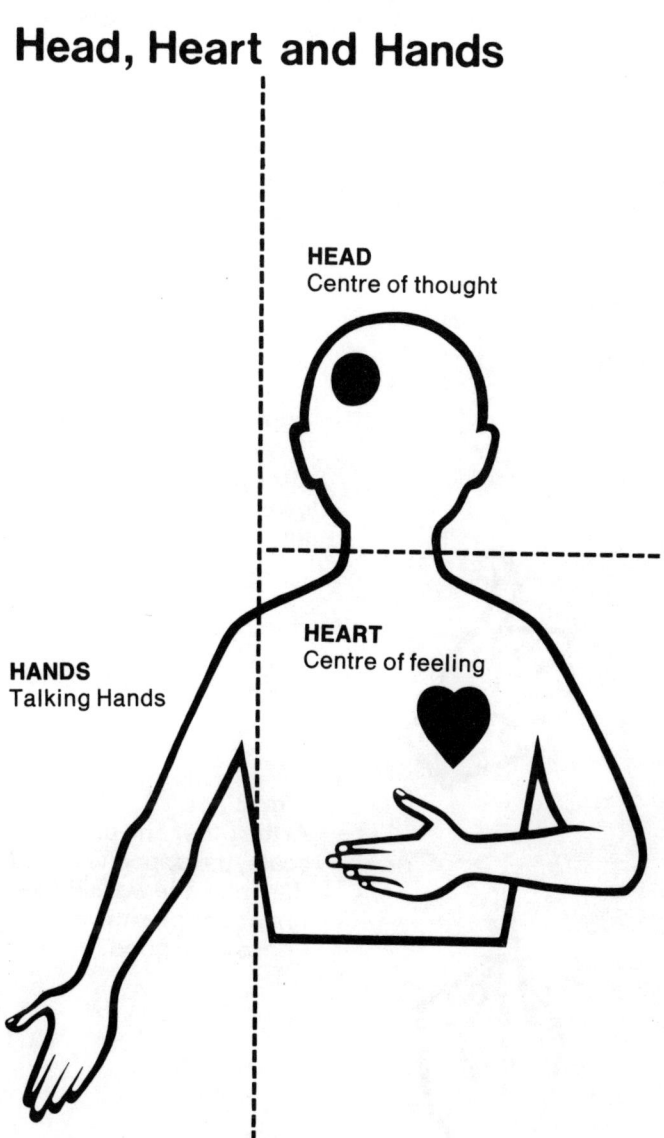

HEAD
Centre of thought

HEART
Centre of feeling

HANDS
Talking Hands

Sign 1 *good*
The thumb, sticking up strongly, known the world over for everything being all right.

Sign 2 *bad*
At the other end of the scale, the opposite end of the hand, the weak little finger denotes the opposite to good.

Sign 3 *how are you?*
What you are really asking here is 'Body good?' in a combination of two signs. The first one indicates the body itself, followed by the sign for 'Good' as in Sign 1, and the enquiring look you give shows it is a question. The same two signs accompanied by an affirming nod indicates 'Body good', or, more conversationally, 'I'm very well!'

Sign 4 *where?*
The right hand, palm uppermost, makes a circular movement, as if looking around for something.

21

Sign 5 *I/me*
This is a perfectly natural gesture, with the index finger of the right hand pointing to yourself.

Sign 6 *you*
An equally natural gesture, the index finger pointing this time to the other person.

Sign 7 *my/mine*
This is similar to 'I' and 'me' although the fist is now closed, as if holding something, to show possession.

Sign 8 *to know*
The thumb makes the sign for 'good', with the tip touching the right temple.

Sign 9 *to like*
The palm of the right hand pats your chest, near to the heart, to show some degree of affection.

Sign 10 *how much?*
The thumb of the right hand rubs across the first two fingers as it 'counts money' on to the open palm of the left hand.

Sign 11 · Numbers 1-10

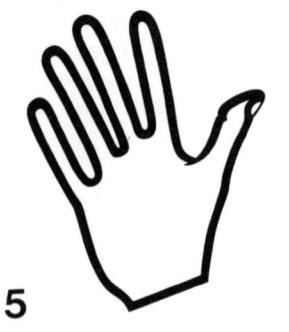

1

2

3

4

Be careful not to confuse this with 'bad'.

5

6

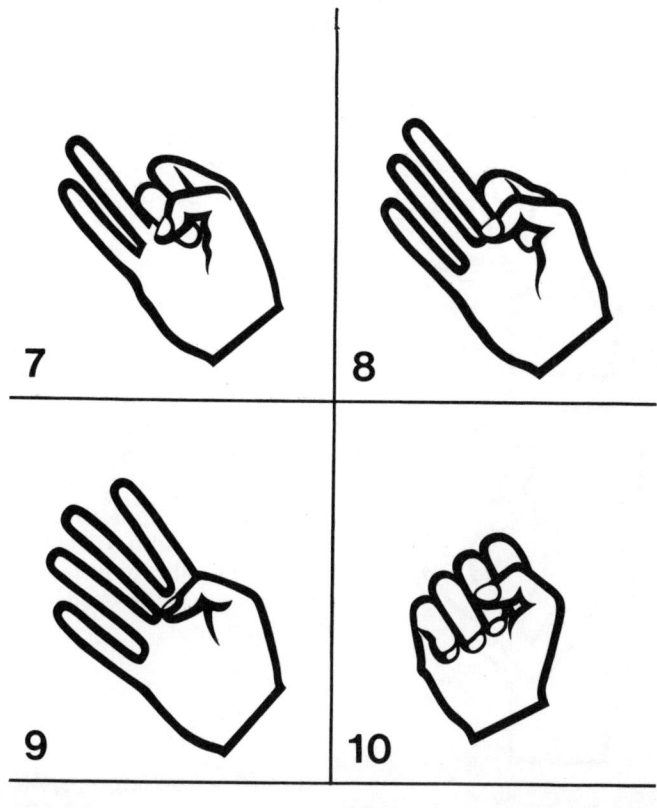

7

8

9

10

Sign 12 £
When counting in pounds sterling, this is indicated by the fingers coming away from the mouth, as they show the number required.

Sign 13 *new pence*
Since the introduction of decimalisation, the finger symbols for 'N' and 'P' have become accepted as the sign for 'new pence'.

Sign 14   *please*
The fingers of the right hand come away from the mouth, in a slow, supplicant gesture, the hand being open, almost as if it were begging for alms.

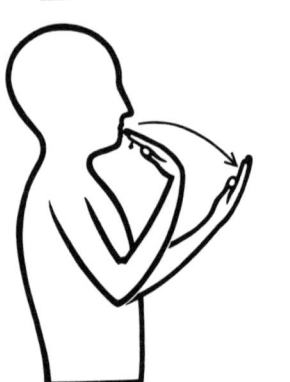

Sign 15   *thank you*
This begins the same way as 'please', but the hand comes down much quicker and stiffer, and in a shorter movement, with an air of finality to it, showing that the request has been met.

Sign 16   *to finger-spell*
The fingers start in the letter 'B' position, and then open and close together rapidly, to indicate talking fingers.

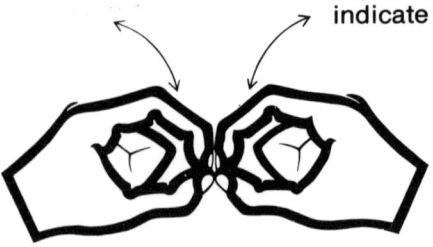

Sign 17 *to sign*
The hands are held a few inches apart, facing each other, and each moves in a circle away from you, passing the message from you, the sender, to the receiver.

Head, Heart and Hands

Signs made by the Talking Hands in conjunction with the Head:

to know
please
thank you

Signs made by the Talking Hands in conjunction with each other:

to finger-spell
to sign
good
bad
where?
you
how much?
Numbers 1–10
£
new pence

Signs made by the Talking Hands in conjunction with the Heart:

to like
how are you?
I/me
my/mine

HAND TALK

In normal conversation, we listen, but now we also have to learn to look. If you can get together with a friend, you can take turns both as a finger-speller and signer, and also as a reader of both. At first, you will probably find that reading is the more difficult of the two, and so the following exercises should be of help.

1. Finger-spell the following words:

architect	jonquil	sociology
barnacle	kitten	technology
confidential	loquacious	university
damage	metabolism	versimilitude
ecology	natural	wheelbarrow
flattery	optical	xenomorphic
geology	personable	yielding
hardship	questionnaire	zeolite
insipid	rheumatism	

2. In the following questions and answers, use signs for the words which are in **bold type**, and finger-spell those for which this is indicated. There are a number of other words which have been added to make them read more naturally, but these are not essential.

Q: **Please, you like new pence?**
A: Yes, **new pence** are **good.**

Q: Do **you like to finger-spell?**
A: **I like to finger-spell.**

Q: Do **you like my** hat? *(Finger-spell 'hat')*
A: **I like** the hat.

Q: Do **you know how much?**
A: **I know.** £4.9 n.p.

Q: Do **you like** giraffes? *(Finger-spell 'giraffes')*
A: **I like** elephants. *(Finger-spell 'elephants')*

Conversation 2

ANN, *a young deaf copy-typist, has just moved with her family to* DAVID GRAY'S *area. As she is not happy with her job, she naturally calls upon him, to see if he can help her. The meeting takes place in his office, and, as before,* DAVID *both speaks aloud and signs when he talks.*

DAVID: Good **morning. What** is **your name?**

ANN: My name is Ann Best.

[*She finger-spells her name, and* DAVID *starts making notes.*]

DAVID: **Ann Best. Can** I **help** you?

ANN: I **want to tell** you **now** I **live** in your **town.**

DAVID: Where in town?

ANN: 9 High Street.

[*Again,* ANN *finger-spells the name of the street.*]

DAVID: 9 High Street. **With** your **family?**

ANN: [*Nods*] Yes.

[*She takes a photograph of her family from her hand-bag and passes it to him.* DAVID *looks and points to the people on it.*]

DAVID: I **see.** Is this your **father?**

[ANN *nods.*]

Mother . . . ? **Brother** . . . ? **Sister** . . . ? You . . . ?

ANN: Yes, me.

[DAVID *gives her the photograph back.*]

DAVID: Thank you. What is their **work?**

ANN: Father . . . **Joiner.**

[DAVID *repeats this after her, making notes as he does so.*]

Mother . . . at **home**

Brother . . . at **school**

Sister . . . **Machinist.**

DAVID: Are your mother **and** father **deaf?**

ANN: [*Shakes her head*] **Hearing. But** my **grandmother** is deaf.

DAVID: Grandmother deaf. She is **old?**

ANN: Yes, old. **Cannot** sign.

[ANN *still hasn't got round to her real reason for calling to see the social worker but their conversation is continued as Conversation 3.*]

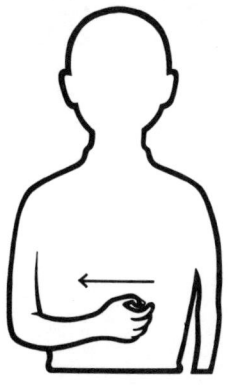

Sign 18　　　　*morning*
The right hand 'draws the
curtain open' moving
across the body from left
to right, near the waist.

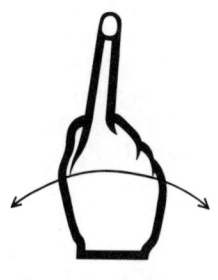

Sign 19　　　　*what?*
The index finger of the
right hand is raised, and
moves from side to side in
an admonishing gesture.
Is it saying 'what-ch
it' . . . ?

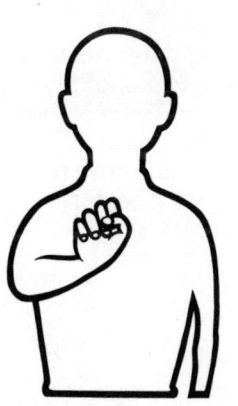

Sign 20　　　　*your*
Just as 'my' is similar to 'I'
except that the hand is
closed to show
possession, so this sign is
similar to 'you' and it is
the closed hand which
points, knuckles
uppermost, to the person
concerned.

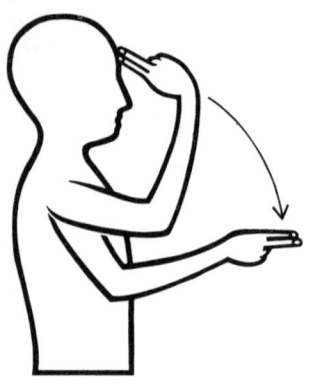

Sign 21 *name*
The right hand makes the letter 'N', not on the left palm, but against the right temple, and then goes away again in a semi-salute.

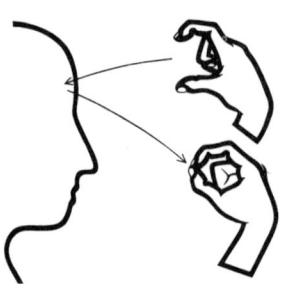

Sign 22 *can*
The right hand makes the letter 'C', goes to the right temple, and then comes away again, the two fingers closing as it does so, as if plucking an idea from the brain and holding on to it.

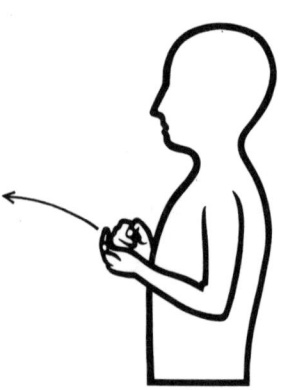

Sign 23 *to help*
The right hand is closed, grasping something, while the palm of the left hand comes up to support it, and they move forward in a giving gesture.

Sign 24 *to want*

The right hand is held high on right side of the chest, and then comes down across the right side of the body, in a short, sharp gesture.

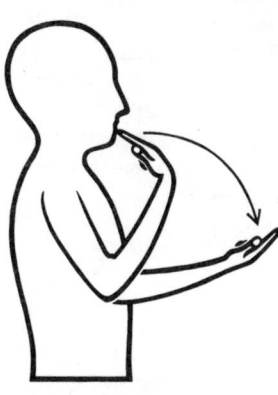

Sign 25 *to tell*

The index finger comes forward from the mouth, 'giving out' the message.

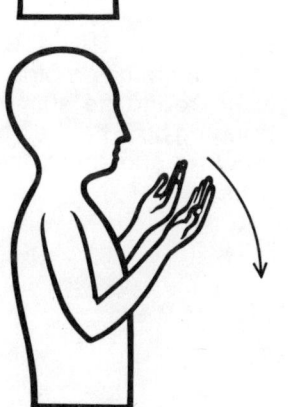

Sign 26 *now*

A two-handed gesture in which the palms of both hands turn uppermost and then come down firmly in an emphatic indication of time.

Sign 27 *to live*
The second finger goes to the chest and moves up and down over the heart, showing liveliness.

Sign 28 *town*
The two hands touch at the finger tips to make the roof and shape of a house, and then move around to show many houses.

Sign 29 *with*
The right hand enfolds itself around the left, bringing both hands together, showing a oneness.

Sign 30 *family*
Another enfolding gesture, in which the hands begin with the palms forward and the tips of the thumbs touching. They then make a circular gesture to come together again, making up the family circle.

Sign 31 *to see*
A perfectly natural gesture, the index finger coming forward from the eye.

Sign 32 *father*
The finger symbol for 'F' repeated twice.

Sign 33 *mother*
The finger symbol for 'M' repeated twice.

35

Sign 34 *brother*
A rubbing together of the knuckles of both hands. Is this the friction between Cain and Abel?

Sign 35 *sister*
The index finger makes a curve, similar to the first part of a written 'S', and moves down the bridge of the nose, not quite to the tip.

Sign 36 *to work*
The right hand is held stiffly above the wrist of the left hand, and then hits it with almost a karate chop, to bounce off again in a forward motion.

Sign 37 _joiner_

The hands move across the body from right to left, as if holding a joiner's plane.

Sign 38 _home_

The right hand makes a waving gesture at the side of the body. Is this mother waving goodbye to her little boy, as he sets out from home?

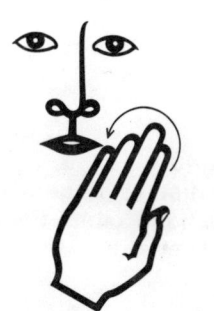

Sign 39 _school_

The back of the right hand is held to the left of the mouth, where it makes a circular gesture, in an anti-clockwise direction. Is this wiping the blackboard clean?

Sign 40 _machinist_

Both hands push forward, palms downwards, as if feeding some material into a machine.

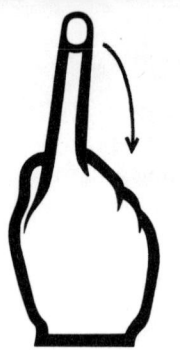

Sign 41 *and*
The index finger of the
right hand starts in a
horizontal position, and
then turns through a
semi-circle to the right, to
include something extra.

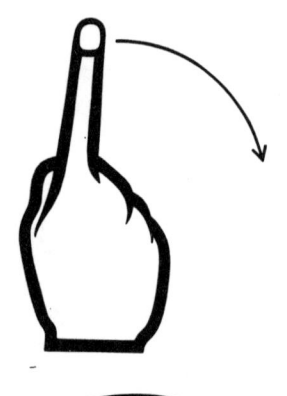

Sign 42 *but*
The index finger starts in
exactly the same position
as before, but this time
makes a short flicking
motion as if cutting off
anything more.

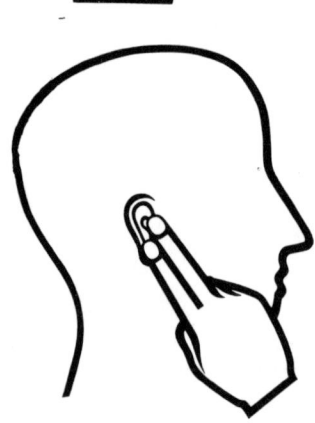

Sign 43 *deaf*
The first two fingers of the
right hand 'close' the
right ear.

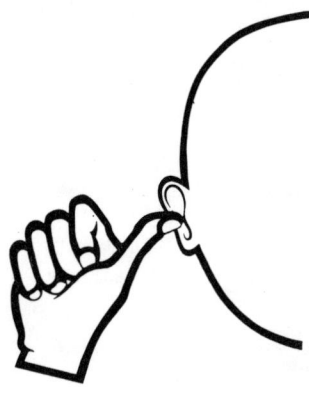

Sign 44   *hearing*
The thumb of the right
hand makes the sign for
'good' at the ear.

Sign 45   *grandmother*
The finger symbol for 'G'
followed by the symbol
for 'M' repeated twice.

Sign 46   *old*
The first two fingers of the
right hand start just below
the eyes, and make a
drawing-out gesture. Are
they drawing attention to
the bags under the eyes?

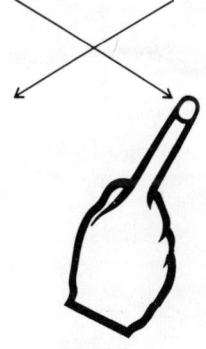

Sign 47   *cannot*
The index finger makes a
crossing-out gesture in
the air, going down from
right to left on the 'can',
and then down from left to
right on the 'not'.

Head, Heart and Hands

Signs made by the Talking Hands in conjunction with the Head:

to tell	school
to see	home
can	deaf
name	hearing
sister	old

Signs made by the Talking Hands in conjunction with each other:

to work
to help
town
family
father
mother
brother
grandmother
joiner
your
now
with
and
but
cannot

Signs made by the Talking Hands in conjunction with the Heart:

to want
to live

Hand talk

In the following questions and answers, again use signs for the words which are in **bold type**, and finger-spell those for which this is indicated. As in all our conversations, there are a number of other words which have been added to make them read more naturally, but, as these are not essential when you are signing, there is no need to include them.

Q: **Can I help you?**
A: Yes, **please. I want to work.**

Q: **Where** do **you want to work?**
A: **I want to work with my brother.**

Q: **Where** does **your father work?**
A: **My father cannot work. My father** is **old.**

Q: **Where** does **your brother work?**
A: **My brother works** in the shipyard. *(Finger-spell 'ship-yard')*

Q Is he a **machinist?**
A: No, he is a **joiner.**

Conversation 3

The young deaf copy-typist, ANN BEST, *has just moved to the town for which* DAVID GRAY *is the Social Worker with the Deaf. After some preliminary 'chat' about her family, at last she gets round to the real reason for her visit to* DAVID's *office.*

DAVID: Oh, I **forgot**. Your work?

ANN: Copy-**Typist**.

   [ANN *mimes typing.*]

   It's **new** work.

DAVID: **How many** work there?

ANN: Five **men** . . . two **women** . . . one **boy** . . . six **girls**.

DAVID: You like your job?

ANN: **No.**

DAVID: **Why?**

ANN: **Because** I'm **bored**.

DAVID: Bored? **Why** . . . ?

ANN: **Yesterday** . . . **today** . . . **tomorrow** . . . **same,** same, same.

DAVID: Tell me.

ANN: Every **day**, **boss gives** me **long lists**. I type in morning. In **afternoon**, no work.

DAVID: You've **asked** your boss for **more** work?

   [ANN *shakes her head.*]

ANN: No, he's **busy**.

DAVID: **Shall** I **talk** to him?

ANN: Yes, please.

DAVID: I will **telephone** him.

ANN: **When** . . . ?

DAVID: Tomorrow.

ANN: Thank you.

Sign 48   *to forget*
The thumb and second finger make the shape of the written letter 'O' and come to touch the temple. As they start to move away again, they flick open, and whatever they had encircled has gone.

Sign 49   *to type*
Miming typing on the up and down plane. If the hands went sideways, it would be playing the piano.

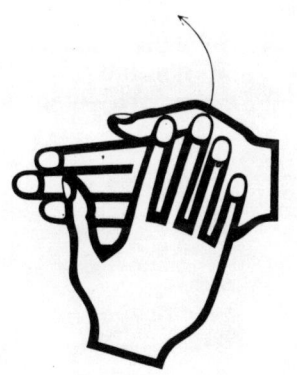

Sign 50   *new*
This is a very quick movement. The left hand is held across the body, and the palm of the right hand passes over the back of it, and suddenly appears over it. Like a jack-in-the-box suddenly popping into sight?

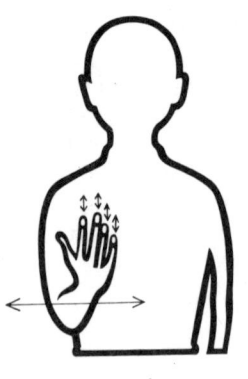

Sign 51 *how many?*
The right hand moves from side to side, while the fingers flick up and down, as if counting heads.

Sign 52 *man*
The thumb and index finger stroke the shape of a beard on the chin.

Sign 53 *woman*
The side of the index finger strokes the smoothness of a woman's cheek.

44

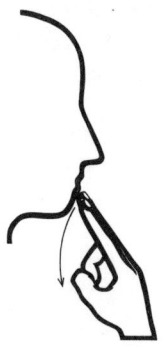

Sign 54 *boy*
The first two fingers touch the chin just below the lips and, then, because there is no beard, they flick down and away from its smoothness. An alternative is to make the sign for 'man' with the right hand, while the left indicates height, or lack of it.

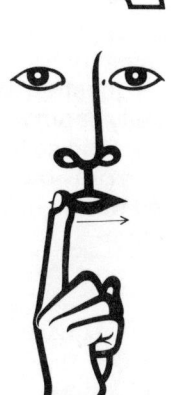

Sign 55 *girl*
The index finger makes a tiny sideways movement, brushing the lips. Is this indicating the soft small lips of a girl? Again, as an alternative, the right hand can make the sign for 'woman' while the left indicates height.

Sign 56 *no/not*
An entirely natural gesture, with the hands starting in a crossed position, and then opening with a wiping-out motion.

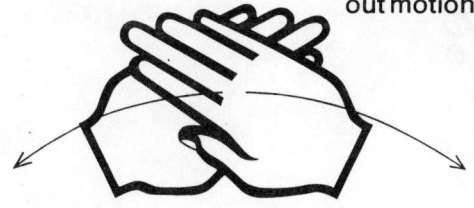

Sign 57 *why?*
The right hand, with the
index finger raised,
comes across the body to
the left arm-pit in one
quick movement, forming
the top of the written
letter 'Y'.

Sign 58 *because*
The answer to the
previous question 'Why?'
will usually begin with
'because', and so this
sign is the previous one
repeated twice in quick
succession.

Sign 59 *bored*
A natural gesture, the
right hand going to the
mouth to stifle a yawn.

Sign 60 _tomorrow_

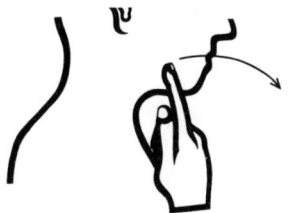

The inside of the index finger touches the right cheek down towards the jawline, and then sweeps forward to meet the day that's coming.

Sign 61 _yesterday_

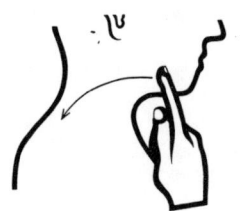

This time, the inside of the index finger touches the same position on the cheek and then curves away towards the shoulder, as if indicating the day that's over.

Sign 62 _today_

The sign for 'now' is repeated twice in quick succession for stress.

Sign 63 *same*
The two index fingers are held together, stressing their similarity.

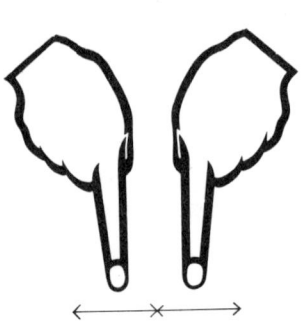

Sign 64 *different*
The index fingers begin in the 'same' position, but then move away from each other, showing a difference between the two.

Sign 65 *day*
The hands are crossed over the eyes, palms inwards, and right over left. They then sweep away in two curves, opening the curtains and letting in the light into the eyes. This can also be the sign for 'light'.

Sign 66   *night*
This is the exact reverse
of day, the hands coming
in to cover the eyes and
shutting off the light. This
can also be the sign for
'darkness'.

Sign 67   *boss*
The admonishing index
finger goes up slightly,
just above and forward of
the right shoulder,
indicating a higher
authority.

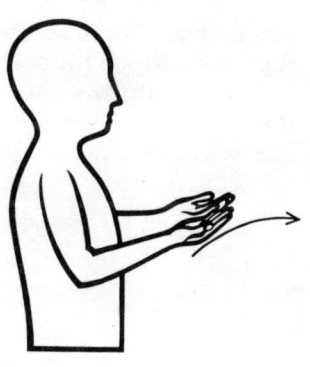

Sign 68   *to give*
The two hands are held
close together, palms
uppermost as if
supporting something.
They then move forward if
you are doing the giving,
but back towards you if
you are asking for
something to be given to
you.

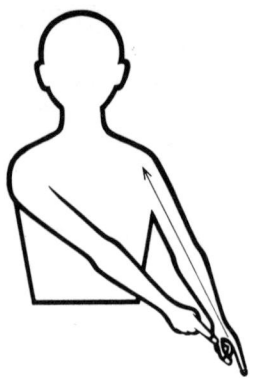

Sign 69   *long*
The index finger of the
right hand travels up the
left arm, from the hand to
the shoulder, indicating
length.

Sign 70   *list*
The thumb of the right
hand moves up and down
the columns of an
imaginary list, checking
off as it does so.

Sign 71   *afternoon*
The first two fingers of the
right hand touch the chin,
before curving away to
the right.

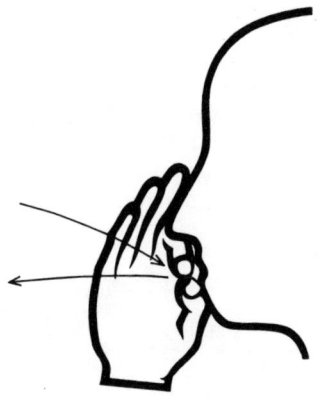

Sign 72   *to ask*
The thumb and index finger of the right hand make a circle, come to the mouth, and then move away again, towards the person to whom you're talking.

Sign 73   *more*
The left hand is held in a slightly cupped position, palm towards the body, and then the palm of the right hand taps against the back of the left, as if adding more to it.

Sign 74   *busy*
The sign for 'work' is repeated very quickly and agitatedly.

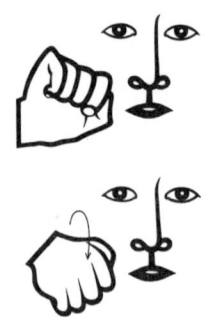

Sign 75   *shall/will*
The clenched fist is held with the knuckle of the index finger touching the cheek, and then it's turned in a clockwise direction, pivoting on this knuckle, as if turning a key.

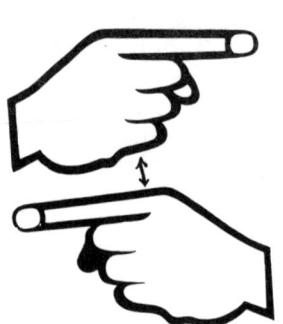

Sign 76   *to talk*
Both hands are clenched apart from the index fingers, and then the right hand goes on top of the left, making the shape of the letter 'X'. In this position, it moves up and down, in a definite, chattering movement.

Sign 77   *telephone*
The thumb and little finger make up the shape of a telephone, and are held to the mouth and ear as if the instrument were real.

Sign 78 *when?*
The three middle fingers of the right hand flutter against the right cheek.

Hand talk

Here is another conversation for you to practise with a friend, taking it in turns to be A and B. As before, a combination of signing and finger-spelling will be needed.

A: Do **you like** the theatre? (*Finger-spell 'theatre'*)
B: **No, I** am **bored.**

A: **But** do **you know** the **Deaf** Theatre?
B: **No.** Is it **different?**

A: Yes. Do **you know why?**
B: Do the **men and women finger-spell and sign?**

A: Yes. **Will you see** the **new** play **with me?** (*Finger-spell 'play'*)
B: **Thank you. Tomorrow night?**

A: **Good. Shall I telephone** the box-office? (*Finger-spell 'box-office'*)
B: **Please. But how much?**

A: **I don't know.**
B: **I see. Will you tell me tomorrow morning?**

Head, Heart and Hands

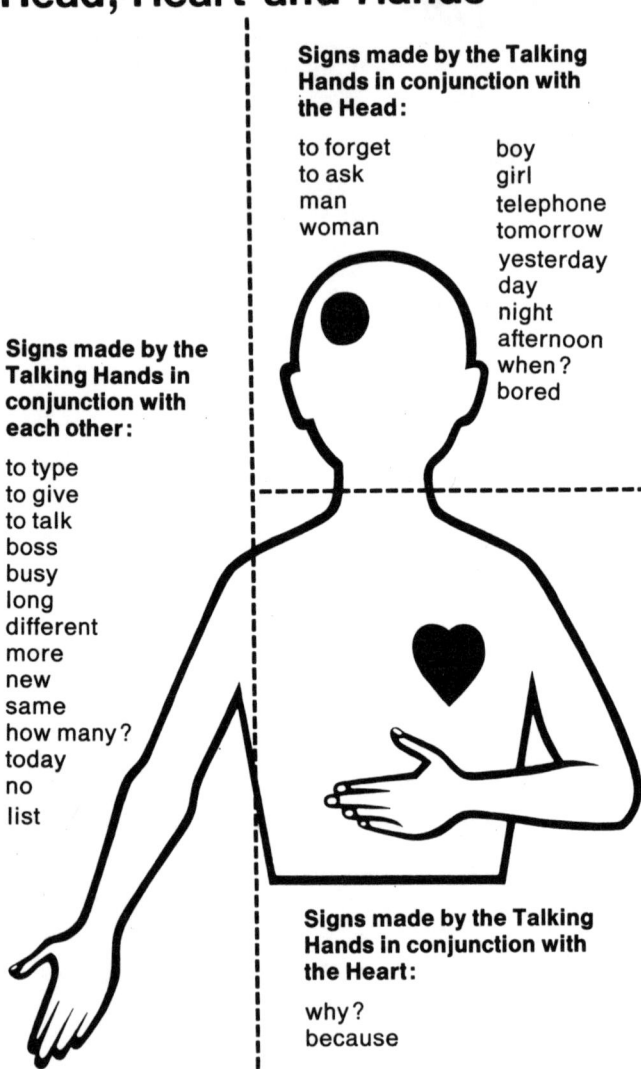

Signs made by the Talking Hands in conjunction with the Head:

to forget
to ask
man
woman

boy
girl
telephone
tomorrow
yesterday
day
night
afternoon
when?
bored

Signs made by the Talking Hands in conjunction with each other:

to type
to give
to talk
boss
busy
long
different
more
new
same
how many?
today
no
list

Signs made by the Talking Hands in conjunction with the Heart:

why?
because

Conversation 4

Deaf people often prefer to do their shopping in a supermarket or self-service store, where everything is on display and there is no need for speech. ANN BEST, *however, has found a small shop where the assistant,* JANE, *has a deaf brother. Because of this,* JANE *is able to sign, and, when* ANN *goes shopping, a lot of chit-chat is exchanged before the actual shopping begins.*

JANE: Good morning, Ann.

[*She finger-spells the name.*]

How are you?

ANN: Well.

JANE: Good. I saw your sister **last week**. She told me she is getting **married next month**.

ANN: Yes.

[*She suddenly sees that* JANE *is wearing an engagement ring.*]

I see you're **engaged. Who** is it?

JANE: Don't be **inquisitive**! [*laughs*]

ANN: You **understand** signs good!

JANE: I understand signs a **little**. What you want **to buy**?

ANN: **Bread** please.

[JANE *puts a sliced loaf on the counter.*]

JANE: **Sliced**. I remember.

ANN: You're **clever**.

JANE: Thank you.

ANN: 1 **lb. Tea** . . . 2 lb. **Sugar** . . . ½ lb. **Butter** . . . **Jam** . . . **Biscuits** . . . **Cake**

[*As* ANN *asks for each item,* JANE *puts it on the counter and also says what it is.*]

JANE: You want 1 lb. **Sausage**?

ANN: Yes, please. Same as last week.

[JANE *puts sausage on the counter.*]

JANE: Sausage. Same as last week.

ANN: **Tin** of **milk**.

[*By mistake,* JANE *puts a tin of cream, and* ANN *realises the error.*]

Not **cream** . . . milk!

JANE: Oh, I am **stupid**!

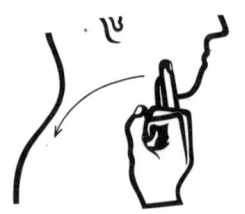

Sign 79 *last week*

In many ways, this is similar to the sign for 'yesterday'. The right hand makes the finger symbol for '7', the days in a week, touches the right cheek, and then curves away backwards towards the shoulder, indicating the seven days that are gone.

Sign 80 *next week*

The right hand again makes the finger symbol for '7', touches the right cheek, but this time it moves forward, indicating the seven days which are to come.

Sign 81 *next month*

The right hand makes the finger symbol for '1', touches the left palm to make the finger symbol 'M' for 'month' – or finger-spells the word in full – and then moves forward as '1' again, to indicate the month that is to come.

Sign 82   *to be engaged*
The first three fingers of
the right hand 'flutter'
over the wedding-finger
of the other hand,
simulating the sparkle of
the stone.

Sign 83   *to marry*
The right hand mimes the
putting-on of the ring on
the wedding-finger, and
then its palm comes down
over the back of the left
hand. Is this the priest
blessing the union?

Sign 84   *my husband*
Since the person talking
is obviously a woman, she
will make the sign for 'my'
and then touch her
wedding ring.

Sign 85   *my wife*
Similar to the above, a
man will make the sign for
'my' and then touch the
wedding-finger,
indicating the ring.

57

Sign 86 *who?*
While the lips are pursed, making the 'oo' sound, the thumb of the right hand touches the chin, just below the mouth, while the index finger points at an angle towards the left.

Sign 87 *inquisitive*
The index finger of the right hand touches the tip of the nose twice, indicating 'nosey parker'

Sign 88 *to understand*
The index finger of the right hand touches the temple in a crooked position, and, as it moves away again, it flicks forward to 'stand' upright.

Sign 89 *little*
The thumb and index finger of the right hand are held close together, to measure a small quantity.

Sign 90 *to buy*
The right hand mimes the lifting of money off the left palm, and then handing it over in exchange for goods.

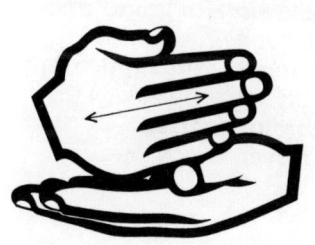

Sign 91 *bread*
The outstretched palm of the left hand supports a loaf of bread, while the right hand, held stiff, is the bread-knife, cutting off a slice.

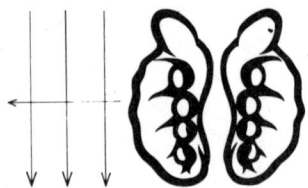

Sign 92 *sliced*
Both hands are held together, their palms almost touching, and then, as the left one remains stationary, the right 'cuts' slices off it.

Sign 93 *to remember*
The right hand clenches itself into a fist on the right temple, and stays there. Is it holding on to an idea?

Sign 94 *clever*
The right thumb makes the sign for 'good' and sweeps across the temple, from right to left. Does good work by the brain produce cleverness?

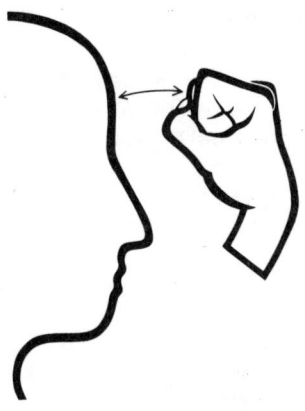

Sign 95　　　　　　　*stupid*
The clenched fist hits
against the temple. Is it
trying to knock some
sense in?

Sign 96　　*pound (weight)*
Make the finger symbols
for 'L' and 'B'.

Sign 97　　　　　　　½
This is similar to the sign
for 'bread' but, this time,
the right hand – the knife –
cuts the palm of the left
hand into two parts, in a
short, sharp movement.

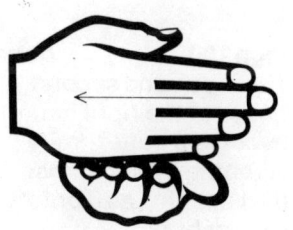

Sign 98 *tea*
The right hand mimes lifting the tea-cup off the saucer of the left palm, in a genteel movement.

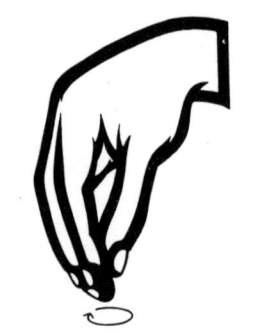

Sign 99 *sugar*
The right hand is held with the fingers bunched and pointing downwards. They then 'sprinkle' sugar from this position.

Sign 100 *butter*
The index and second finger of the right hand become a butter-knife, scraping butter across the left palm, as if onto a slice of bread.

Sign 101 *jam*
The right hand wipes away the last traces of jam and stickiness from the mouth, while the tongue licks the middle finger clean.

Sign 102 *biscuits*
With the left arm bent, so that the hand is near the left shoulder, the right hand cups itself around the left elbow, and then strikes it three or four times. Does this date back to the days of sail, when ships biscuits had to be broken against something hard?

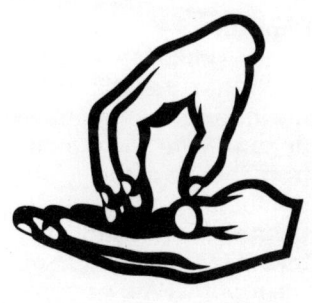

Sign 103 *cake*
The right hand is held over the palm of the left, the tips of the fingers and thumb just touching, so that it takes up the approximate shape of a cup-cake.

63

Sign 104 *sausage*
Both hands are held in front of the body, and then move to left and right, clenching and unclenching as they go, measuring off the links in a string of sausages.

Sign 105 *tin*
Both hands are held palms together, the right over the left. They then measure off between them the size of the tin container.

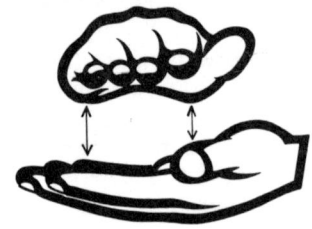

Sign 106 *milk*
Both hands mime the action of hand-milking a cow.

Sign 107 *cream*
This is similar to the sign for 'butter' but, this time, the index and second fingers 'skim' the cream from the top of the container of milk, the palm of the left hand, and take it in the direction of the mouth. Who's been licking the cream?

Head, Heart and Hands

Signs made by the Talking Hands in conjunction with each other:

to buy
to be engaged
to marry
husband
wife
bread
sliced
pound (weight)
½
tea
sugar
butter
biscuits
cake
sausage
milk
cream
jam
tin
little
next month
two months ago

Signs made by the Talking Hands in conjunction with the Head:

to understand who?
to remember inquisitive
last week clever
next week stupid

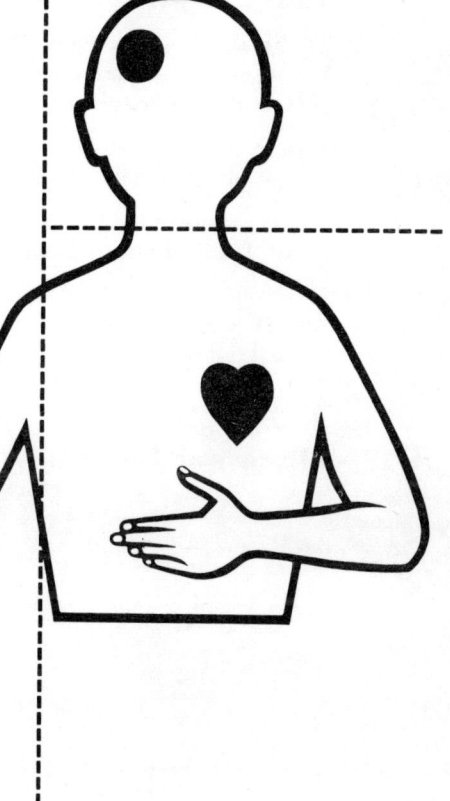

Hand talk

As before, you can practise both signing and finger-spelling in the following conversation, concerning some succulent sausages.

A: **Please, tell me . . . where** did **you buy** those **sausages?**
B: The **sausages I gave you last week?**

A: **You remember? You** are **clever.**
B: Those **sausages** were **good. My brother liked** them.

A: **My husband likes** them. He's **asking** for **more.**
B: **I bought** the **sausages** in the delicatessen in **town.**
(*Finger-spell 'delicatessen'*)

A: **Where** in **town?**
B: **7** Low Street. (*Finger-spell name of street*)

A: **I will remember. 7** Low Street.
B: **Shall I telephone** the shop **tomorrow?** (*Finger-spell 'shop'*)

A: **Thank you! Please.**
B: **I shall ask** for **3 lb.**

A: **Why 3 lb?**
B: **½ lb.** for **me** . . . **1 lb.** for **my brother. ½ lb.** for **you** . . . **1 lb.** for **your husband.**

Conversation 5

By now, ANN BEST *has her new job, and is thinking of going on holiday with a friend who is also deaf. As often happens in situations like this, when precise details have to be arranged, she has asked* DAVID GRAY *to meet her at the travel agent's, so he can help her. But, just like a woman,* ANN *is a little late.*

ANN: I'm **sorry** I'm **late**. I couldn't catch a **bus** because of the **rain**.

DAVID: That's **all right**. I was **early**.

[*He indicates the brochures he's been glancing at while he waited.*]

I **read** about **holidays** in the **sun**. You **look** at them.

[*As* ANN *sits down to look at the brochures,* DAVID *goes to talk to the girl behind the counter.*]

This young lady wants to arrange a holiday for her friend and herself.

ASSISTANT: Yes, sir. Where does she want to go?

DAVID: I'll find out the details in a moment.

[*He goes to join* ANN *as she glances at the brochures.*]

Where do you want **to go? England** . . . ?
Germany . . . ?

ANN: No, too **cold**.

DAVID: **Paris, France?**

ANN: No, I want sun.

DAVID: **Italy . . . ? Spain . . . ?**

ANN: I **choose Spain.**

DAVID: Will you go by **train** and **boat**, or by **plane**?

ANN: My **friend** is **afraid** of the **ocean**. We'll go by plane.

DAVID: You must be **rich**.

ANN: No, we're **poor**. We **save**.

DAVID: You want to buy **tickets** now?

ANN: Yes, please.

DAVID: All right, I'll tell the girl.

[*He stands and goes to where the assistant is waiting.*]

Sign 108   *to be sorry*
The little finger of the
right hand makes the
symbol for 'bad' and then
goes to the heart, where it
makes a circular
movement. Do we feel sad
at heart because of
something bad?

Sign 109   *late*
The left palm becomes a
clock face, the end of the
thumb representing
twelve o'clock. The index
finger of the right hand
becomes a hand of the
clock, pointing to twelve
o'clock. From there, it
moves forward towards
six o'clock, showing that
the starting time is
behind, indicating
lateness.

Sign 110   *early*
This begins exactly the
same as the preceding
sign, but this time the
index finger moves back
towards nine o'clock,
showing that the starting
time is still ahead,
indicating earliness.

Sign 111 *bus/car*

Both hands are in front of the body, holding a steering-wheel. If the wheel is a large one, it belongs to a bus, but, if it is small, it belongs to a car.

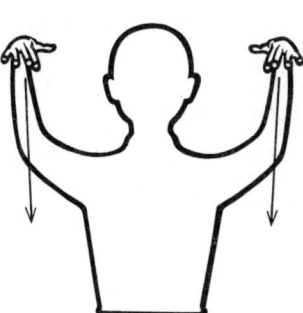

Sign 112 *rain*

Both hands are held in front of the body, palms downwards at head height, and, as they move down, the fingers mime the action of falling rain.

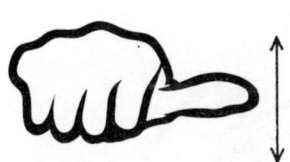

Sign 113 *all right*

The thumb of the right hand makes the 'good' sign, but in a horizontal position in front of the body. It then flicks up and down two or three times, indicating that all is well in the surrounding area.

Sign 114 *to read*
Both hands are held together, palms uppermost in front of the body, simulating an open book, for the eyes to read.

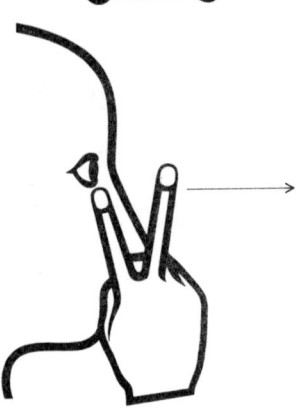

Sign 115 *to look*
This is the same as 'to see' except that two fingers are used, doubling the intensity of the gaze.

Sign 116 *holidays*
The middle fingers of both hands move around happily in the air, expressing buoyancy and freedom.

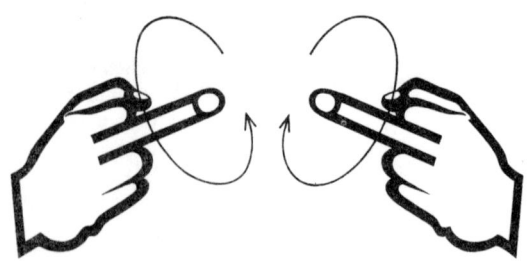

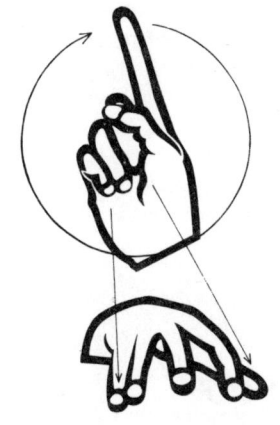

Sign 117   *sun*
The index finger of the
right hand draws the
circle of the sun up in the
air, and then, as the hand
comes down, the fingers
open, to show the rays of
the sun shining down.

Sign 118   *hot*
The back of the right hand
is brushed across the
forehead, going from left
to right, as if wiping away
perspiration, which is
then flicked from the
hand at the end of the
movement.

Sign 119   *cold*
Both hands are clenched
across the chest, as you
mime a shivering action.

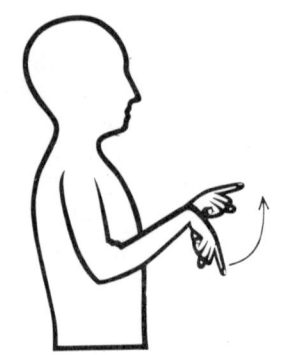

Sign 120 *to go*

The index finger of the right hand is held pointing downwards, and then moves slowly up and away from the body to point forward, indicating a distinct movement to another place.

Sign 121 *England*

The tip of the right index finger goes along the length of the left index finger towards the tip, back to where it started, and then back along again. Is this an association with 'E' for England, or is it the navy firing its big guns at England's enemies?

Sign 122 *Spain*

For this, you simply mime the action of clicking castanets in a Spanish dance.

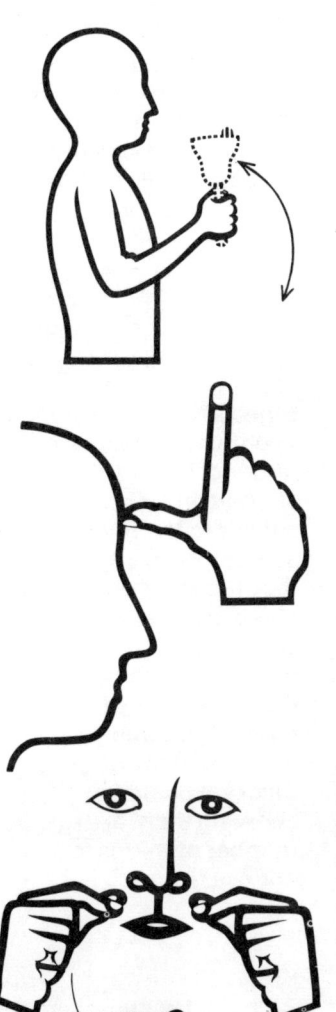

Sign 123 *Italy*
The right hand holds onto a hand-bell and rings it. Is this an old-fashioned ice-cream salesman drawing attention to his wares?

Sign 124 *Germany*
The thumb and index finger of the right hand make a right-angle, and then the thumb touches the forehead, so that the index finger is upright. Is this the spike on an old-fashioned German helmet?

Sign 125 *France*
Both hands twirl the ends of a waxed moustache, and then the right one strokes the small, pointed beard of a stage Frenchman.

Sign 126 *Paris*
Both hands curve together and go up in the air together, their tips touching to make the shape of the Eiffel Tower.

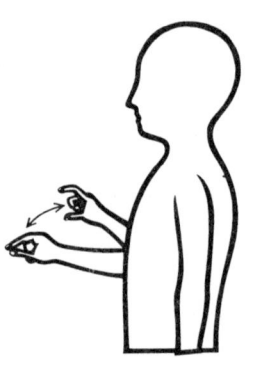

Sign 127 *to choose*
The thumb and index finger of the right hand are held in a position similar to the finger symbol for 'C', and, as they move forward, they close, as if selecting something. This is brought to the body, and then they open again, to repeat the same movement in a slightly different position, showing there are a number of things to choose from.

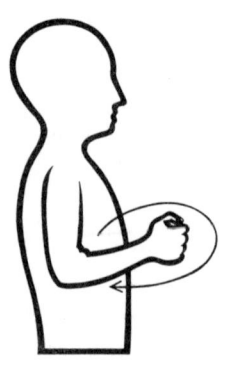

Sign 128 *train*
With the fist clenched, the right hand is held to the side of the body, and then the whole arm makes the movement of an old-fashioned steam piston.

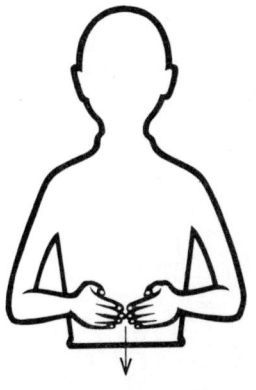

Sign 129 *boat*
The finger-tips of both hands come together in front of the body, to make up the shape of a ship's bow. As they push forward through the water, a few up-and-down movements can be added, to simulate the waves.

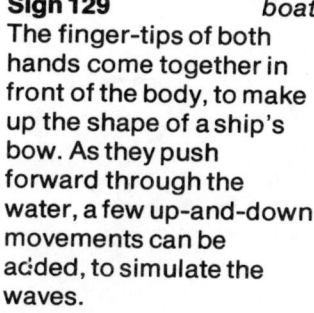

Sign 130 *plane*
This is similar to the sign for 'telephone' but, this time, the thumb and little finger of the right hand are the wings of an aeroplane, as the hand itself flies through the air.

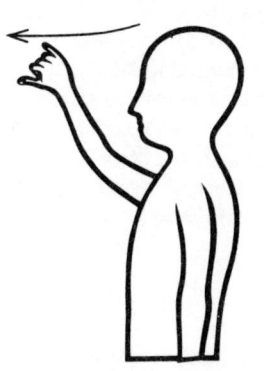

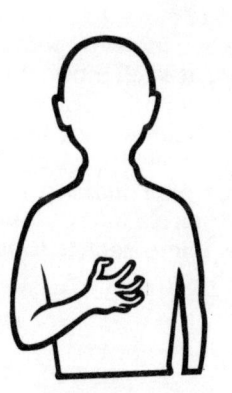

Sign 131 *to be afraid*
The right hand in clawed position beats against the chest twice, as the body shrinks away from it.

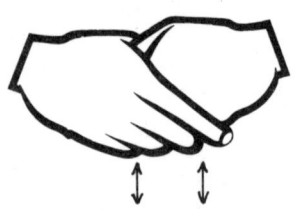

Sign 132 *friend*
The two hands clasp each
other, right over left, and
then shake in friendship.

Sign 133 *ocean*
The hands are held palms
downwards, the right
above the left, and, as
they move together from
left to right, they simulate
the up-and-down motion
of the waves.

Sign 134 *we/us*
The two index fingers
point at each other, their
tips touching, 'you' and
'me' together, and then
they go away from each
other, each making a
semi-circle in the air until
they come back to touch
the body.

Sign 135 *rich*
Both hands are held slightly curved, both little fingers touching the chest, and then they move down the body in a slow, sweeping gesture, almost making the shape of the written letter 'V'. Are they drawing attention to the richness of one's apparel?

Sign 136 *poor*
The right hand 'scratches' the left elbow, drawing attention to either the hole that is there, or the patched garment.

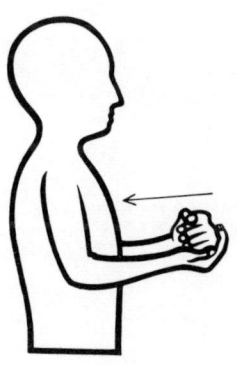

Sign 137 *to save*
The right hand is held in a cupped position on the palm of the left, and they move together towards the body with a gathering-in movement.

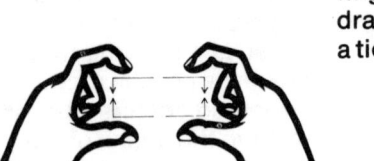

Sign 138 *ticket*
The thumb and index
fingers of the two hands
draw the oblong shape of
a ticket in the air.

Head, Heart and Hands

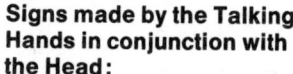

Signs made by the Talking Hands in conjunction with the Head:

to look	Germany
sun	France
hot	

Signs made by the Talking Hands in conjunction with each other:

to read
to go
to choose
ticket
bus/car
rain
holiday
England
Spain
Paris
Italy
train
boat
plane
friend
ocean
poor
early
late
all right

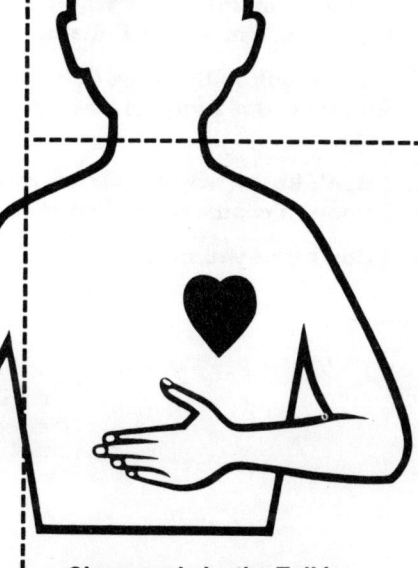

Signs made by the Talking Hands in conjunction with the Heart:

to be sorry	cold
to be afraid	rich
to save	we/us

Hand talk

This time, the conversation takes the form of some mild domestic bickering.

A: **Where** is the **butter**?
B: **I'm sorry. I don't know.**

A: **But you bought butter yesterday.**
B: **I know. I chose** the **butter you like.**

A: **You chose French butter?**
B: Yes, **I bought 2 lb.**

B: **Please, remember . . . where** is it?
B: **I'm sorry. I'm afraid I'm stupid. I don't know!**

A: **Shall I look** in the fridge? (*Finger-spell 'fridge'*)
B: **All right. But I looked this afternoon.** It's **not** in the fridge.

A: **I don't know why I married you.**
B: **I know. Because you liked me.**

A: **I don't like you now!**

Conversation 6

By now, ANN *has returned home from her holiday in Spain. When she is in a snack-bar with* MAY, *the friend who went on holiday with her,* DAVID GRAY *catches sight of her. He brings his cup of coffee over to their table, and asks if he may join them.*

DAVID: Can I **sit** here?

   [*The two girls nod and* DAVID *sits down.*]

   Were you **happy** on holiday, Ann?

ANN: Yes, thank you. But my friend was **disappointed**.

DAVID: Why?

MAY: The **food** gave me a **pain**.

DAVID: Very bad?

MAY: Yes, I saw the **doctor**.

DAVID: The doctor? Did he give you **medicine**?

MAY: Yes, **Tablets**.

DAVID: You'll have **to take care** if you go **next year**.

ANN: I'll go again next year.

DAVID: You like Spain?

ANN: Yes, I like the sun and **wine**.

DAVID: And the **boys**?

ANN: The boys were **cheeky**. I **laughed**.

DAVID: But your friend was **sad**?

ANN: Not **always. Sometimes**, very happy.

DAVID: Why?

ANN: She liked one Spanish boy.

DAVID: Was it **difficult** to talk to the boy?

ANN: No, **easy**. A little signing.

   [DAVID GRAY *takes no further part in the conversation, as the two girls sign to each other.*]

MAY: **Be quiet.**

ANN: Why? You **love** the Spanish boy?

MAY: [*to* DAVID] She is **envious** of me!

ANN: That's not **true**.

MAY: I'm only **teasing**!

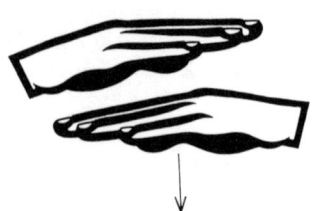

Sign 139 *to sit*
Both hands are held palms downwards, with the right about two inches above the left. Together, they move down a short distance in a sharp movement.

Sign 140 *happy*
Both hands are held slightly cupped, and then they come together in a clapping movement, with the right hand doing most of the work.

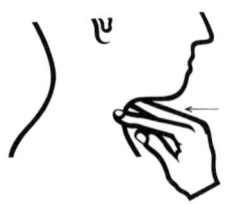

Sign 141 *to disappoint*
The index and second finger of the right hand make a 'V', and go either side of the throat in a quick, cutting movement.

Sign 142 *food*
The right hand makes up its part of the finger symbol 'B', and then mimes the carrying of food to the mouth.

Sign 143 *pain*
The right hand is held with the fingers hanging limply. It is then shaken two or three times, while the face takes on a pained expression.

Sign 144 *doctor*
The right hand comes across the left hand, to take its pulse just as a doctor would.

Sign 145 *medicine*
The left hand is cupped, to form an apothecary's mortar, while the little finger of the right hand becomes the pestle, which goes round the mortar two or three times in a clockwise direction, crushing the ingredients inside.

Sign 146 *tablets*
The index finger of the right hand makes a tiny circle on the outstretched palm of the left, tracing the shape of a tablet.

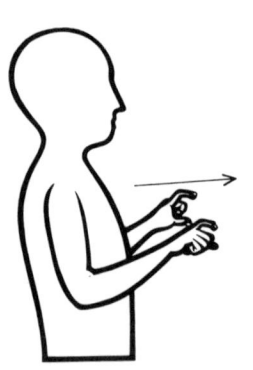

Sign 147 *to take care*
Both hands form the finger symbol 'C', and then point towards the person you are telling to take care.

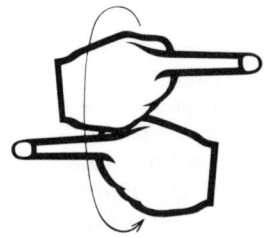

Sign 148 *next year*
The right hand, with its index finger pointing to the left, rests on top of the left hand, with its index finger pointing to the right. The right hand then circles away from the body, under the left hand, and then resumes its former position. In some areas, this action is done by the two index fingers alone.

Sign 149 *last year*
The hands begin in exactly the same position as above, but, this time, the right hand moves towards the body and then under the left.

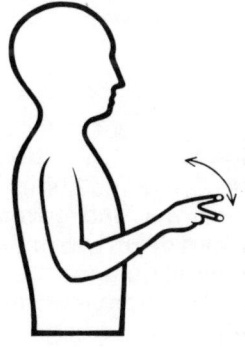

Sign 150 *again*
The index and second finger of the right hand make a 'V', and then move backwards and forwards two or three times, suggesting the repetition of an action.

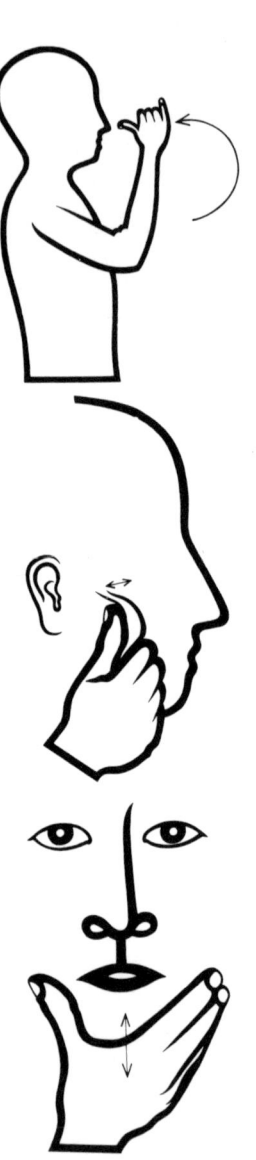

Sign 151   *wine*

The thumb and little finger of the right hand become the top of a Spanish *poron,* and this goes to above the mouth in an exaggerated circular gesture, so that wine can be poured down to the waiting mouth. As the thumb is in the 'good' position, does this also indicate that the vintage is excellent?

Sign 152   *cheeky*

The thumb and index finger of the right hand pinch the right cheek and shake it, stressing the cheekiness.

Sign 153   *to laugh*

The right hand holds the chin firmly, and moves it up and down two or three times, simulating the chin's action when one laughs.

Sign 154   *sad*
With the palm slightly curved, the right hand comes down over the face, from forehead to chin, 'wiping on' a sad expression. Is this connected with the putting on of the Greek mask of tragedy?

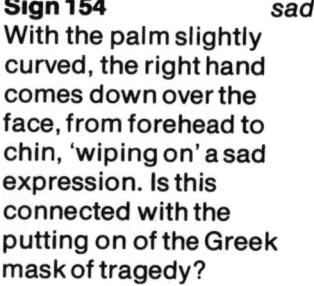

Sign 155   *always*
The right hand is clenched, and its knuckles push upwards on the palm of the left hand, travelling from the wrist to the tips of the fingers and beyond.

Sign 156   *sometimes*
This is in two parts. First, the right hand is clenched, as if holding something, and then the thumb 'measures out' small quantities of whatever this is, indicating 'some'. This is followed by the left palm becoming a clock face, and the index finger of the right hand one of the clock hands. This points first at twelve o'clock, and then moves round to about three o'clock, indicating 'time'.

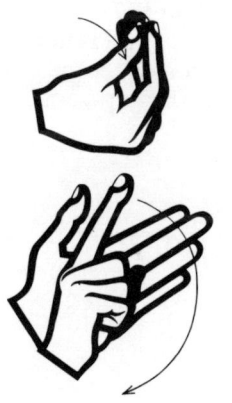

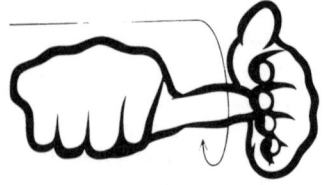

Sign 157 *difficult*

The thumb of the right hand goes to the outstretched palm of the left, and presses there, the hand twisting as it does so. At the same time, the face has a pained expression. Is the palm so hard that the thumb is finding it difficult to make an impression?

Sign 158 *easy*

The right cheek is inflated a little, and the index finger of the right hand taps it twice.

Sign 159 *to love*

Both hands and arms cross over the chest in an embracing action.

Sign 160   *to be quiet*
The palm of the right hand touches the mouth, and, as it moves outwards, it turns and the fingers snap together, indicating that the mouth should do the same.

Sign 161   *envious*
The right hand is held slightly clenched, and then is 'clawed' across the top part of the chest, from left to right. Is the body being torn apart by envy and jealousy?

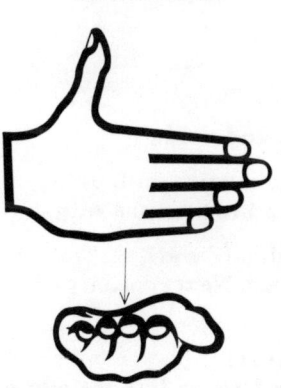

Sign 162   *true*
The left hand is held palm uppermost, and then the right hand comes down directly from above it, drawing a straight and true line in the air, before it hits the left palm with almost a karate chop. At the same time, the right thumb is making the sign for 'good'. Everything is good and true.

89

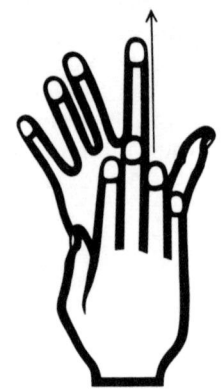

Sign 163 *to tease*
The index finger of the left hand points to the person doing the teasing, and then the right hand, also pointing to the person, brushes over the finger two or three times.

Hand talk

As we near the end of our book, what better topic to discuss than holidays.

A: Have **you** a **new car?** (*Finger-spell 'have'*)
B: **No, I** have an **old car, but** it's **good.**

A: Do **you go** on **holiday** in the **car?**
B: Yes, **I like car holidays.**

A: **Where** did **you go last year?**
B: **England, but I went early.**

A: Was it **all right?**
B: **No, bad. Seven days rain and cold.**

A: **I know.** It's **difficult when** it **rains** on **holiday.**
B: That's **true!** It's **not easy to laugh** in the **rain.**

A: Do **you go** on **holiday with** a **friend?**
B: **Sometimes, but not last year. Next year, my brother and sister will go with me.**

A: **Where will you go next year?**
B: To **Spain. My brother and sister like** the **sun and wine.**

90

Head, Heart and Hands

Signs made by the Talking Hands in conjunction with the Head:

to disappoint	wine
to laugh	cheeky
to be quiet	sad
food	easy

Signs made by the Talking Hands in conjunction with each other:

to sit
to tease
pain
doctor
medicine
tablets
difficult
true
happy
next year
last year
again
always
sometimes
to take care

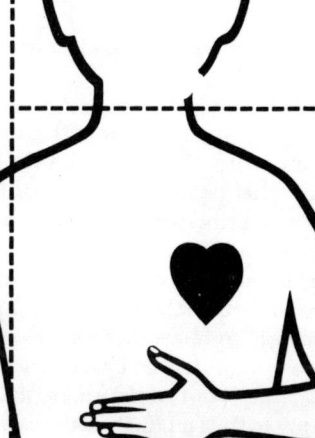

Signs made by the Talking Hand in conjunction with the Heart:

to love
envious

Goodbye to Talking Hands . . . ?

We sincerely hope not!

By the time you have reached this part of our book, you should have learned, memorised and absorbed most of the signs you have been reading about; and, no doubt, you will also have watched the Tyne Tees Television series on which this book is based. But what really counts is putting into practice what you've been learning, so do make every effort to meet deaf people, and do your best to hold a conversation with them. Sometimes, you might find that some of their signs are slightly different from yours, but don't let that worry you! You are still learning, and, perhaps, so are they . . . ! But it is *together* that you will be able to accomplish so much.

That is the whole object of TALKING HANDS, to enable hearing people to get together with people who are deaf, and communicate with them at a level they will understand. Don't forget that people with normal hearing like ourselves have a great number of words stored away in our minds, while people with impaired hearing have a far lesser store. This is due to the fact that only by listening as we are growing up have we learned all these words. And it is by listening, too, that we are able to reproduce the sound of the words. Many deaf people whom you will meet will have speech which is easily understood, but, with others, the opposite is true. This is due simply to the fact that people can only 'echo' the speech that they hear, and so, the greater the degree of deafness, the greater the difficulty in reproducing the exact sounds. In time, however, and by constantly meeting people who are deaf, you will come to understand them more easily . . . and, naturally, they will also come to understand you better, too.

Above all, never forget that people who are deaf are *people*! They have all the joys, ambitions, sorrows, worries, desires, agonies, happiness and expectations that we all share as members of the human race. By going along with us this far, you have shown your awareness of this, and your interest in the problems of those who are deaf. Please, don't let this die away . . . ! As a next step, why not contact one of your local voluntary organisations for the deaf, to see how you can help further, or find out from the Social Services Department of your local authority, where the nearest club for deaf people is, and volunteer your services there.

In any cases of difficulty, drop a line to either of these organisations:

The Royal National Institute for the Deaf
105 Gower Street
LONDON WC1E 6AH

The British Deaf Association
38 Victoria Place
CARLISLE CA1 1EX

These are both large, voluntary organisations working on behalf of and for people who are deaf, and they will be happy to give you all the necessary information.

And, in conclusion, let us remember that the old saying 'Many hands make light work', is never truer than when the hands are TALKING HANDS!

Vocabulary

Figures immediately after the words refer to the Sign Numbers used in this book.